THAT ROCKS!

EARTH'S MINERALS

By Maria Nelson

Gareth Stevens
Publishing

Please visit our website, www.garethstevens.com. For a free color catalog of all our high-quality books, call toll free 1-800-542-2595 or fax 1-877-542-2596.

Library of Congress Cataloging-in-Publication Data

Library of Congress Cataloging-in-Publication Data

Nelson, Maria.
Earth's minerals / Maria Nelson.
     p. cm. — (That rocks!)
Includes index.
ISBN 978-1-4339-8310-8 (pbk.)
ISBN 978-1-4339-8311-5 (6-pack)
ISBN 978-1-4339-8309-2 (library binding)
1. Minerals—Juvenile literature. 2. Earth—Juvenile literature. I. Title.
QE365.2.N45 2014
549—dc23

                                            2012047094

First Edition

Published in 2014 by
Gareth Stevens Publishing
111 East 14th Street, Suite 349
New York, NY 10003

Copyright © 2014 Gareth Stevens Publishing

Designer: Katelyn Londino
Editor: Kristen Rajczak

Photo credits: Cover, p. 1 Olga Miltsova/Shutterstock.com; p. 5 afitz/Shutterstock.com; p. 7 commons.wikimedia.org/wiki/File:Quartz_vein_cape_jervis.jpg/Wikipedia.org; p. 9 Stockbyte/Thinkstock.com; p. 11 Martin Novak/Shutterstock.com; p. 13 Anneka/Shutterstock.com; p. 15 commons.wikimedia.org/wiki/File:Streak_plate_with_Pyrite_and_Rhodochrosite.jpg/Wikipedia.org; pp. 17, 19 (main) Terry Davis/Shutterstock.com; p. 19 (inset) commons.wikimedia.org/wiki/File:Hope_Diamond.jpg/Wikipedia.org; p. 20 (inset) © iStockphoto.com/joebelanger.

Printed in the United States of America

CPSIA compliance information: Batch #CS13GS: For further information contact Gareth Stevens, New York, New York at 1-800-542-2595.

CONTENTS

Words in the glossary appear in **bold** type the first time they are used in the text.

3

BREAKING IT DOWN

What do diamonds and salt have in common? Though they may look different to you and have very different uses, diamonds and salt are both minerals! A mineral is **inorganic**. It's a homogenous solid, which means it has the same **chemical** makeup throughout. Making a mineral smaller by **physical** means, such as cutting it in half, won't change its properties.

Minerals have been forming underground for billions of years. There are more than 3,000 different minerals found on Earth—and scientists are discovering more all the time!

SET IN STONE

Rocks are made of one or more minerals.

Quartz, the shiny matter in this rock, is a common mineral.

FORM FROM CHANGE

Minerals form under all sorts of physical and chemical conditions, such as changing temperature and pressure. There are several main ways for minerals to form.

Some minerals form when melted rock from deep within Earth rises to the surface and cools. Others form when weather, especially wind and water, wears down rock and causes matter to settle and harden into new forms. New conditions can cause minerals to form from other minerals, too.

SET IN STONE

Scientists can make minerals in labs that are almost exactly the same as those that formed naturally. However, since they didn't form in nature, these aren't considered true minerals.

Minerals form in cracks, or veins, found in rock when hot water mixtures from within Earth flow into them.

WHAT'S INSIDE?

Scientists can **identify** minerals using tools that magnify them or look inside them. Each mineral is made up of atoms arranged in a special, repeating **pattern**. These atoms come from two or more elements. Scientists can tell what mineral they're seeing by what elements are present and how the atoms are arranged.

From color to shape, the elements and atomic arrangement of a mineral establish its properties. Humans have a repeating pattern that tells our bodies how to look, too—it's called DNA!

SET IN STONE

"Atom" is the general term for the most basic unit of all matter. Elements are kinds of atoms that have features individual to that element.

Minerals are divided into groups based on their chemical makeup. Some of these include sulfides, silicates, and halides.

CRYSTALS

In the right conditions, we're able to see a mineral's orderly atoms in a beautiful way—crystals! While minerals aren't alive, scientists say their crystals "grow" because they branch out underground, somewhat like a plant's roots. Many mineral crystals take thousands of years to fully form. Salt, however, can grow crystals quickly!

Finding a recognizable crystal can be hard since many minerals don't have enough space for crystal growth. They're also often next to another mineral, and their crystals may grow into each other.

SET IN STONE

Sometimes, animals can form minerals! For example, an oyster's shell is partly made of organically produced aragonite.

The look of a mineral's crystal can be one way to identify it.

A QUICK LOOK

People who study and collect minerals can often tell what kind of mineral they have found just by looking at it. How much light can be seen through a mineral, or its transparency, is one recognizable feature. A mineral's **luster** is noticeable, too. Minerals can be said to be "metallic" or "pearly," meaning their shine looks like metal or pearls.

Transparency and luster can aid in identifying a mineral at a glance. However, other physical properties can tell one mineral from another with more certainty.

SET IN STONE

Mineraloids, a group that includes mercury and opal, are often studied along with minerals. However, they lack one or more common mineral properties, such as crystal growth.

Graphite, pictured here, is a mineral with no transparency. It's opaque, which means no light can pass through it.

ANIMAL, VEGETABLE, OR MINERAL?

One way to identify a mineral is by hardness, or its ability to withstand scratching. Scratching it with increasingly hard minerals tests this. When the mineral shows a scratch, it can be placed on the hardness scale, which helps figure out what mineral it is.

Streak, or the color of a mineral when it's crushed to powder, is another easily tested property. A mineral is rubbed on a piece of tile. The color of powder it produces helps identify the mineral.

SET IN STONE

The Mohs scale of mineral hardness orders minerals from 1—the softest minerals—to 10. The higher a mineral's number on the scale, the fewer minerals can scratch it.

The tiles that minerals are rubbed on for the streak test are called streak plates. A streak plate has a hardness of about 7, so some minerals are too hard to streak!

Color can be helpful in figuring out which mineral you have. Gold, for example, is always close to the same color.

But some minerals can be many colors! This may be because of the presence of a very small amount of an element, such as the iron that makes clear quartz turn purple. It's then called amethyst! Since color can also change with strong heat or light, properties other than color are better to use in identifying a mineral.

SET IN STONE

Some minerals are part of a series. That means the number of elements in their chemical makeup differs slightly from one mineral example to the next. This can change the color!

Azurite contains the element copper, which gives it a blue-green color.

SO MANY USES

From copper used in making wires to silica-based computer chips, we have found many uses for Earth's minerals. Limestone and aluminum can be used for building. Airplanes may be made of titanium! Many minerals are worth a lot of money, either because they're useful or because they're hard to find.

Did you know **jewelry** is made of minerals? Gold and silver are commonly melted and made into rings and necklaces. Some pieces are decorated by gemstones, which are simply cut and polished crystals!

SET IN STONE

One of the most famous gems is the Hope Diamond. You can see this 45.52-**carat** diamond at the Smithsonian National Museum of Natural History in Washington, DC.

Hope Diamond

Since minerals are often found deep underground, companies build **mines** in order to find them.

19

MINERAL SEARCH

Many people like to collect minerals. Since they can form in all kinds of conditions, collectors all over the world can often find many different minerals near where they live.

Many years ago, collectors searched mines for minerals. That can be unsafe. Today, only workers or mine owners are allowed into a mine. Everyone else needs special permission. However, collectors also often find minerals at construction sites, along the edges of roads, or in other places where digging occurs.

SET IN STONE

When a new mineral is found, it may be named for its color, where it was found, the person who found it, or a famous person.

IDENTIFYING COMMON MINERALS

name	color	streak	hardness
copper	red-orange; turns green-blue in air	red-orange	2½–3
diamond	colorless, yellow, brown, black, blue, green, red, pink, tan	too hard to streak	10
graphite	black, gray	black, gray	1–2
halite	colorless, whitish, yellow, red, purple, blue	white	2½
quartz	colorless, purple, red, black, yellow, brown, green, blue, orange	white	7

GLOSSARY

carat: measure of weight of gems. Five carats is equal to 1 gram (0.035 oz).

chemical: relating to matter that can be mixed with other matter to cause changes

identify: to find out the name or features of something

inorganic: being made of matter other than plant and animal

jewelry: pieces of metal, often holding gems, worn on the body

luster: the glow created by reflected light

mine: a pit from which minerals are taken

pattern: the way colors or shapes happen over and over again

physical: having to do with natural science

FOR MORE INFORMATION

Books

Hyde, Natalie. *What Are Minerals?* New York, NY: Crabtree Publishing, 2012.

Squire, Ann. *Minerals.* Danbury, CT: Children's Press, 2013.

Websites

How Rocks & Minerals Are Formed
www.rocksforkids.com/RFK/howrocks.html
Read about the formation of rocks and minerals, and find links to other related topics.

Mineralogy 4 Kids
www.mineralogy4kids.org/
Play games and learn more about rocks and minerals.

Photo Gallery: Minerals
science.nationalgeographic.com/science/photos/minerals/
See pictures and read about many kinds of minerals found on Earth.

INDEX